A BOOK OF AMERICANS

Christopher Columbus

A BOOK
OF
AMERICANS

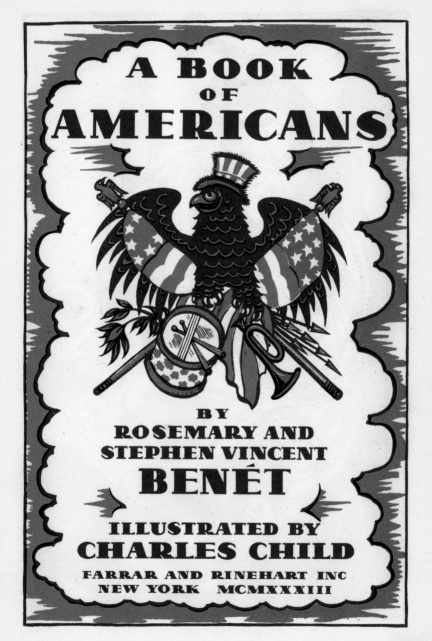

BY
ROSEMARY AND
STEPHEN VINCENT
BENÉT

ILLUSTRATED BY
CHARLES CHILD

FARRAR AND RINEHART INC
NEW YORK   MCMXXXIII

CONTENTS

CONTENTS

To
Stephanie, Thomas, and Rachel
our other works in collaboration

APOLOGY

We couldn't put in all the great
Or even all the small,
And many names with sterling claims
We haven't used at all.

But here's a rather varied lot,
As anyone can see,
And all and each by deed and speech
Adorned our history.

Some got the medals and the plums,
Some got their fingers burnt,
But every one's a native son,
Except for those who weren't.

So praise and blame judiciously
Their foibles and their worth.
The skies they knew were our skies, too,
The earth they found, our earth.

A BOOK OF AMERICANS

CHRISTOPHER COLUMBUS

1446?-1506

There are lots of queer things that discoverers do
But his was the queerest, I swear.
He discovered our country in One Four Nine Two
By thinking it couldn't be there.

It wasn't his folly, it wasn't his fault,
For the very best maps of the day
Showed nothing but water, extensive and salt,
On the West, between Spain and Bombay.

There were monsters, of course, every watery mile,
Great krakens with blubbery lips
And sea-serpents smiling a crocodile-smile
As they waited for poor little ships.

There were whirlpools and maelstroms, without any doubt
And tornadoes of lava and ink.
(Which, as nobody yet had been there to find out,
Seems a little bit odd, don't you think?)

But Columbus was bold and Columbus set sail
(Thanks to Queen Isabella, her pelf),
For he said "Though there may be both monster and gale,
I'd like to find out for myself."

And he sailed and he sailed and he *sailed* and he SAILED,
Though his crew would have gladly turned round
And, morning and evening, distressfully wailed
"This is running things into the ground!"

But he paid no attention to protest or squall,
This obstinate son of the mast,
And so, in the end, he discovered us all,
Remarking, "Here's India, at last!"

He didn't intend it, he meant to heave to
At Calcutta, Rangoon or Shanghai,
There are many queer things that discoverers do.
But his was the queerest. Oh my!

INDIAN

I don't know who this Indian is,
A bow within his hand,
But he is hiding by a tree
And watching white men land.
They may be gods—they may be fiends—
They certainly look rum.
He wonders who on earth they are
And why on earth they've come.

He knows his streams are full of fish,
His forests full of deer,
And his tribe is the mighty tribe
That all the others fear.
—And, when the French or English land,
The Spanish or the Dutch,
They'll tell him they're the mighty tribe
And no one else is much.

They'll kill his deer and net his fish
And clear away his wood,
And frequently remark to him
They do it for his good.
Then he will scalp and he will shoot
And he will burn and slay
And break the treaties he has made
—And, children, so will they.

We won't go into all of that
For it's too long a story,
And some is brave and some is sad
And nearly all is gory.
But, just remember this about
Our ancestors so dear:
They didn't find an empty land.
The Indians were *here*.

HERNANDO DE SOTO

1499?-1542

Hernando De Soto was Spanish,
An iron-clad *conquistador*.
Adventure he knew in the sack of Peru,
But it just made him anxious for more.

Hernando De Soto was knightly,
Hernando De Soto was bold,
But like most of his lot, he'd be off like a shot
Wherever he heard there was gold.

So, with priest and physician and army,
Not to speak of a number of swine,
At Tampa he started a quest, fiery-hearted,
For the gold of a fabulous mine.

And from Florida way out to Texas,
This Don of the single-track mind,
Went chasing his dream over prairie and stream,
And the pigs kept on trotting behind.

He discovered the great Mississippi,
He faced perils and hardships untold,
And his soldiers ate bacon, if I'm not mistaken,
But nobody found any gold.

They buried De Soto at midnight,
Where the wide Mississippi still jigs.
He was greedy for gain but a soldier of Spain.
(I hope someone looked after the pigs.)

PEREGRINE WHITE AND
VIRGINIA DARE

1620   1587

Peregrine White
And Virginia Dare
Were the first real Americans
Anywhere.

Others might find it
Strange to come
Over the ocean
To make a home,

England and memory
Left behind—
But Virginia and Peregrine
Didn't mind.

One of them born
On Roanoke,
And the other cradled
In Pilgrim oak.

Rogues might bicker
And good men pray.
Did they pay attention?
No, not they.

Men might grumble
And women weep
But Virginia and Peregrine
Went to sleep.

They had their dinner
And napped and then
When they woke up
It was dinner again.

They didn't worry,
They didn't wish,
They didn't farm
And they didn't fish.

There was lots of work
But they didn't do it.
They were pioneers
But they never knew it.

Wolves in the forest
And Indian drums!
Virginia and Peregrine
Sucked their thumbs.

They were only babies.
They didn't care.
Peregrine White
And Virginia Dare.

POCAHONTAS

1595?-1617

Princess Pocahontas,
Powhatan's daughter,
Stared at the white men
Come across the water.

She was like a wild deer
Or a bright, plumed bird,
Ready then to flash away
At one harsh word.

When the faces answered hers,
Paler yet, but smiling,
Pocahontas looked and looked,
Found them quite beguiling.

Liked the whites and trusted them,
Spite of kin and kith,
Fed and protected
Captain John Smith.

Pocahontas was revered
By each and every one.
She married John Rolfe
She had a Rolfe son.

She crossed the sea to London Town
And must have found it queer,
To be Lady Rebecca
And the toast of the year.

"La Belle Sauvage! La Belle sauvage!
Our nonpareil is she!"
But Princess Pocahontas
Gazed sadly toward the sea.

They gave her silks and furbelows.
She pined, as wild things do
And, when she died at Gravesend
She was only twenty-two.

Poor wild bird—
No one can be blamed.
But gentle Pocahontas
Was a wild thing tamed.

And everywhere the lesson runs,
All through the ages:
Wild things die
In the very finest cages.

MILES STANDISH

1584-1656

Miles Standish was a little man, a soldier from his youth,
He said he'd fought the Spaniards and I think he told the
truth,
For he could fire a musketoon and he could build a fort
And the Pilgrims all admired him, though he wasn't quite
their sort.

Tom Morton was a merry man and liked a merry frolic
He said, "These long-nosed Pilgrims give an honest heart the
colic!"
He built a place called Merry Mount to serve his merry ends
And danced around a Maypole with a lot of rowdy friends.

The Pilgrims were indignant, for they didn't like his game,
They said his merry Maypole was an idol and a shame,
They vowed that it was scandalous to dance to such a tune,
So they ordered out Miles Standish, with his fav'rite musketoon.

"Ho, ho!" laughed Morton, merrily, " 'Tis only Captain
Shrimp!"
"Hew down yon idol!" Standish roared and made him feel
quite limp
For they hewed the pretty Maypole down, in spite of all his
cries,
And chopped it into kindling wood before his very eyes.

They sent him back to England and they told him to stay
there.
—They didn't like gay gentlemen with perfume in their hair.
—They didn't like wild gentlemen with mischief in their port.
But they always liked Miles Standish, though he wasn't quite
their sort.

He lived with them and fought for them and drove their
foes away,
A bold cock-robin of a man whom nothing could dismay,
And, when he died, they mourned him from the bottom of
their hearts.
For it isn't where your inches stop. It's where your courage
starts.

PILGRIMS AND PURITANS

1620

The Pilgrims and the Puritans
Were English to the bone
But didn't like the English Church
And wished to have their own
And so, at last, they sailed away
To settle Massachusetts Bay.

And there they found New England rocks
And Indians with bows on
But didn't mind them half as much
(Though they were nearly frozen)
As being harried, mocked and spurned in
Old England for the faith they burned in.

The stony fields, the cruel sea
They met with resolution
And so developed, finally,
An iron constitution
And, as a punishment for sinners,
Invented boiled New England dinners.

They worked and traded, fished and farmed
And made New England mighty
On codfish, conscience, self-respect
And smuggled aqua-vitae.
They hated fun. They hated fools.
They liked plain manners and good schools.

They fought and suffered, starved and died
For their own way of thinking
But people who had different views
They popped, as quick as winking,
Within the roomy local jail
Or whipped through town at the cart's rail.

They didn't care for Quakers but
They loathed gay cavaliers
And what they thought of clowns and plays
Would simply burn your ears
While merry tunes and Christmas revels
They deemed contraptions of the Devil's.

But Sunday was a gala day
When, in their best attire,
They'd listen, with rejoicing hearts,
To sermons on Hell Fire,
Demons I've Met, Grim Satan's Prey,
And other topics just as gay.

And so they lived and so they died,
A stern but hardy people,
And so their memory goes on
In school house, green and steeple,
In elms and turkeys and Thanksgiving
And much that still is very living.

For, every time we think, "Aha!
I'm better than Bill Jinks,
So he must do just as I say
No matter what he thinks
Or else I'm going to whack him hard!"
The Puritan's in our backyard.

But, when we face a bitter task
With resolute defiance,
And cope with it, and never ask
To fight with less than giants
And win or lose, but seldom yell
—Why, that's the Puritan, as well.

PETER STUYVESANT

1592-1682

What, never seen Nieuw Amsterdam?
That grieves me to the core!
You should have visited the place
In sixteen-sixty-four,
A tidy, little, red-roofed town
With tulip-pots aglow,
And ruled by Peter Stuyvesant
With his famous timber toe.

'Twas all as Dutch as Dutch could be,
Except for dykes and ditches.
The plump Dutch chickens laid Dutch eggs
Among the Dutchman's-breeches,
Even the babies talked in Dutch,
For Dutch was all they knew,
And there walked Peter Stuyvesant
(One leg was wooden, too).

His farm was called The Bouwerie
And there he kept his cow,
Because he was the Governor
(He couldn't do it now).
And he was proud as anything
Of his New Netherlands.
(He had, it's true, a wooden limb
But it had silver bands.)

And all the ruddy-faced *mijnheers*,
And all the neat *mevrouws*
Would greet their peppery overlord·
With genuine Dutch bows.
They liked him for his sturdy pith,
Although he had his whims.
(And then, they liked a governor
With two such different limbs.)

So, when the English fleet sailed in,
One bright September day,
And said "We've come with fife and drum
To take your town away."
He stamped and jumped and swore and thumped
But could not make them run.
(You cannot pit a wooden leg
Against a naval gun.)

But still he kept his Bouwerie
And would his *schnapps* uncork,
Although they took Nieuw Amsterdam
And changed it to New York,
And, to the last, his wooden leg
Would hurt him very much
When he would think about the day
That really beat the Dutch.

SOUTHERN SHIPS AND SETTLERS

1606-1732

O, where are you going, "Goodspeed" and "Discovery"?
With meek "Susan Constant" to make up the three?
We're going to settle the wilds of Virginia,
For gold and adventure we're crossing the sea.

And what will you find there? Starvation and fever.
We'll eat of the adder and quarrel and rail.
All but sixty shall die of the first seven hundred,
But a nation begins with the voyage we sail.

O, what are you doing, my handsome Lord Baltimore?
Where are you sending your "Ark" and your "Dove"?
I'm sending them over the ocean to Maryland
To build up a refuge for people I love.

Both Catholic and Protestant there may find harbor,
Though I am a Catholic by creed and by prayer.
The South is Virginia, the North is New England.
I'll go in the middle and plant my folk there.

O, what do you seek, "Carolina" and "Albemarle",
Now the Stuarts are up and the Roundheads are down?
We'll seek and we'll find, to the South of Virginia,
A site by two rivers and name it Charles Town.

And, in South Carolina, the cockfighting planters
Will dance with their belles by a tropical star.
And, in North Carolina, the sturdy Scotch-Irish
Will prove at King's Mountain the metal they are.

O, what are you dreaming, cock-hatted James Oglethorpe?
And who are the people you take in the "Anne"?
They're poor English debtors whom hard laws imprison,
And poor, distressed Protestants, fleeing a ban.

I'll settle them pleasantly on the Savannah,
With Germans and Highlanders, thrifty and strong.
They shall eat Georgia peaches in huts of palmetto,
And their land shall be fertile, their days shall be long.

All
We're the barques and the sailors, the bread on the waters,
The seed that was planted and grew to be tall,
And the South was first won by our toils and our dangers,
So remember our journeys. Remember us all.

COTTON MATHER

1663-1728

Grim Cotton Mather
Was always seeing witches,
Daylight, moonlight,
They buzzed about his head,
Pinching him and plaguing him
With aches and pains and stitches,
Witches in his pulpit,
Witches by his bed.

Nowadays, nowadays,
We'd say that he was crazy,
But everyone believed him
In old Salem town
And nineteen people
Were hanged for Salem witches
Because of Cotton Mather
And his long, black gown.

Old Cotton Mather
Didn't die happy.
He could preach and thunder,
He could fast and pray,
But men began to wonder
If there *had* been witches—
When he walked in the streets
Men looked the other way.

CAPTAIN KIDD

1650?-1701

This person in the gaudy clothes
Is worthy Captain Kidd.
They say he never buried gold.
I think, perhaps, he did.

They say it's all a story that
His favorite little song
Was "Make these lubbers walk the plank!"
I think, perhaps, they're wrong.

They say he never pirated
Beneath the Skull-and-Bones.
He merely traveled for his health
And spoke in soothing tones.
In fact, you'll read in nearly all
The newer history books
That he was mild as cottage cheese
—But I don't like his looks!

FRENCH PIONEERS
1534-1759

New France, New Spain, New England,
Which will it be?
Who will win the new land?
The land across the sea?

They came here, they toiled here,
They broke their hearts afar,
Normandy and Brittany,
Paris and Navarre.

They lost here, at last here,
It wasn't so to be.
Let us still remember them,
Men from oversea.

Marquette and Joliet,
Cartier, La Salle,
Priest, corsair, gentleman,
Gallants one and all.

France was in their quick words,
France was in their veins.
They came here, they toiled here.
They suffered many pains.

Lake and river, stream and wood,
Seigneurs and dames—
They lived here, they died here,
They left singing names.

OLIVER DE LANCEY
1749-1822

This general in British garb
Is Oliver De Lancey.
They were a noted family
And really very fancy.

They owned large slices of New York,
And quite a lot of Jersey,
But, when the Revolution came,
They all cried out, "Oh mercy!"

"Why this will never, never do!
It is a rebel orgy,
And we are loyal subjects, who
Will fight for good King Georgie!"

And so they did, with might and main,
Though people called them Tories
—And lost their houses and their lands
And all their former glories.

While, if they'd won (which they did not)
We'd still have rulers regal.
No Stars and Stripes! No July Fourth!
No bold American eagle!

It's such a topsy-turvy thought
It gives me indigestion,
But, just remember this: There are
Two sides to every question.

GEORGE WASHINGTON
1732-1799

Sing hey! for bold George Washington,
That jolly British tar,
King George's famous admiral
From Hull to Zanzibar!
No—wait a minute—something's wrong—
George *wished* to sail the foam.
But, when his mother thought, aghast,
Of Georgie shinning up a mast,
Her tears and protests flowed so fast
That George remained at home.

Sing ho! for grave George Washington,
The staid Virginia squire,
Who farms his fields and hunts his hounds
And aims at nothing higher!
Stop, stop, it's going wrong again!
George *liked* to live on farms,
But, when the Colonies agreed
They could and should and would be freed,
They called on George to do the deed
And George cried "Shoulder arms!"

Sing ha! for Emperor Washington,
That hero of renown,
Who freed his land from Britain's rule
To win a golden crown!
No, no, that's what George *might* have won
But didn't, for he said,
"There's not much point about a king,
They're pretty but they're apt to sting
And, as for crowns—the heavy thing
Would only hurt my head."

Sing ho! for our George Washington!
(At last I've got it straight.)
The first in war, the first in peace,
The goodly and the great.
But, when you think about him now,
From here to Valley Forge,
Remember this—he might have been
A highly different specimen,
And, where on earth would we be, then?
I'm glad that George was George.

JOHN PAUL JONES

1770-1850

My mother and my father were as Scotch as Scotch could be
And I lived at Kirkcudbright, by the foam,
But, when I was but twelve years old, they shipped me off to
    sea,
And, since then, I've wandered everywhere but home.

I've been master of a slaver and I've killed my mutineer,
And fled Tobago's law and changed my name,
And there's a bonny rumor I once served a buccaneer,
And, if I did, he found me hard to tame.

But now I sport the Stars and Stripes, and all the British coast,
From Leith to Plymouth Harbor, must beware
Of a new flag flying and a captain like a ghost
Who strikes before their frigates know he's there.

"It's the 'Ranger'!" "It's the devil!" "It's the Yankee, John
    Paul Jones!"
"O, catch him, burn him, sink him!" Let them try!
They shall fish my cousin, Davy, from his sea-horse-guarded
    thrones
Ere they blot my daring topsails from the sky!

My soul for a good frigate! and the tools to match my might
That this landlubber Congress will not give!
Yet I'll take the haughty "Serapis" by moon and cannon-light
With my "Bon Homme Richard" leaking like a sieve.

They'll give me a gold medal and a gold-hilted sword.
They'll make me an admiral and all.
But I'll be off to Russia at Empress Catherine's word,
For roving is my fortune and my fall.

And I'll die worn out in Paris, as they lop King Louis' head,
And my grave shall be forgot a hundred years,
Till another sailor finds it, and they bear me, lapped in lead,
To slumber at Annapolis with my peers.

ABIGAIL ADAMS

1744-1818

If you would be
  Wise or rare,
Pick your grandmother
  With care.

There's no doubt about it,
The Adams were lucky,
For the one that *they* picked
Was both witty and plucky.

She had all of the virtues
And most of the graces,
And believed that all wives
Should stay right in their places.

Now, John had no tact,
But his Abigail did,
A salient fact
Which she tactfully hid.

Alone and unaided,
She raised sons and daughters,
While John went to Congress
Or over wide waters.

She could lord it in London
Or skimp it at home,
And manage both households
With equal aplomb.

For Abigail's metal
Was strong as fine steel,
And Abigail's manners
Exceeding genteel.

Her pride and her cleverness,
All of her treasure,
Were bequeathed to her sons
In a bountiful measure.

This accounts for the Adams,
How then could they fail?
But *what* were the forces
That made Abigail?

JOHN ADAMS

1735-1826

The old rutted roads have been turned to macadams,
But Quincy and Braintree remember the Adams.

There was John and John Quincy, Charles Francis and Brooks
And Henry, who wrote most remarkable books.

And a number of others I will not describe,
But John—this is he—was the first of the tribe.

The son of a farmer, a lawyer by trade,
He was always on hand when our Nation was made.

A statesman of genius, a patriot of zeal,
He was vain as Old Harry but true as cold steel.

He founded our Navy, from rudder to mast,
He saw that the bold Declaration was passed.

But he kept us from war with the French at a time
When to fight would have been little less than a crime.

For he wasn't hot-headed, though stubborn and fiery
And given to writing mean things in his diary.

He served but one term in the President's chair,
And his foes made it hot for him while he was there.

But, at eighty years old, he was still going strong
And convinced that no Adams could ever be wrong.

And his sons and his grandsons and all of his stock
Were chips of the selfsame, identical block.

Remarkable men, with the tart Adams quirk,
And the same Adams talent for doing good work

In spite of the tumult which always arose
When they carefully trod upon other folks' toes.

For their crotchets were theirs, but their virtues the Nation's,
And they served us superbly for four generations.

They could irritate Job, but they never were small.
—And this is John Adams, who started them all.

BENJAMIN FRANKLIN

1706-1790

Ben Franklin munched a loaf of bread while walking down the
  street
And all the Philadelphia girls tee-heed to see him eat,
A country boy come up to town with eyes as big as saucers
At the ladies in their furbelows, the gempmun on their horses.

Ben Franklin wrote an almanac, a smile upon his lip,
It told you when to plant your corn and how to cure the pip,
But he salted it and seasoned it with proverbs sly and sage,
And people read "Poor Richard" till Poor Richard was the
  rage.

Ben Franklin made a pretty kite and flew it in the air
To call upon a thunderstorm that happened to be there,
—And all our humming dynamos and our electric light
Go back to what Ben Franklin found, the day he flew his kite.

Ben Franklin was the sort of man that people like to see,
For he was very clever but as human as could be.
He had an eye for pretty girls, a palate for good wine,
And all the court of France were glad to ask him in to dine.

But it didn't make him stuffy and he wasn't spoiled by fame
But stayed Ben Franklin to the end, as Yankee as his name.
"He wrenched their might from tyrants and its lightning from
  the sky."
And oh, when he saw pretty girls, he had a taking eye!

BENEDICT ARNOLD

1741-1801

While this is a fellow whom few can admire,
For he sold his own country for money and ire,

It is Arnold the brilliant, the wayward and proud,
With a light in his eye like the spark from a cloud;

The reckless of danger, the greedy for fame,
With the black, ineffaceable mark on his name.

He fought like a lion, Quebec to purloin;
He helped win Saratoga from Johnny Burgoyne.

On land and on water, he blazed and he burned
—And was slandered by foes for the laurels he'd earned.

So, half for revenge and the rest in a pet,
He did the black thing we would gladly forget,

And wrote to the British, in characters clear:
"*West Point.*

> X marks my room and I wish you were here."

"Won't you come for a visit? The fort's very nice
And I'll sell you us both for the following price—"

The plot was discovered and Benedict fled
To the British encampment with shame on his head.

They kept to their bargain, as Britons will do,
They paid him and made him a general, too.

But the sword had a tarnish, the money a stain,
And he never was lucky or happy again,

Till he died in dejection, some twenty years later,
For, wherever he went, he was "Arnold the traitor."

THOMAS JEFFERSON

1743-1826

Thomas Jefferson,
What do you say
Under the gravestone
Hidden away?

"I was a giver,
I was a molder,
I was a builder
With a strong shoulder."

Six feet and over,
Large-boned and ruddy,
The eyes grey-hazel
But bright with study.

The big hands clever
With pen and fiddle
And ready, ever,
For any riddle.

From buying empires
To planting 'taters,
From Declarations
To trick dumb-waiters.

"I liked the people,
The sweat and crowd of them,
Trusted them always
And spoke aloud of them.

"I liked all learning
And wished to share it
Abroad like pollen
For all who merit.

"I liked fine houses
With Greek pilasters,
And built them surely,
My touch a master's.

"I liked queer gadgets
And secret shelves,
And helping nations
To rule themselves.

"Jealous of others?
Not always candid?
But huge of vision
And open-handed.

"A wild-goose-chaser?
Now and again,
Build Monticello,
You little men!

"Design my plow, sirs,
They use it still,
Or found my college
At Charlottesville.

"And still go questing
New things and thinkers,
And keep as busy
As twenty tinkers.

"While always guarding
The people's freedom—
You need more hands, sir?
I didn't need 'em.

"They call you rascal?
They called me worse.
You'd do grand things, sir,
But lack the purse?

"I got no riches.
I died a debtor.
I died free-hearted
And that was better.

"For life was freakish
But life was fervent,
And I was always
Life's willing servant.

"Life, life's too weighty?
Too long a haul, sir?
I lived past eighty.
I liked it all, sir."

ALEXANDER HAMILTON
1757-1804

Jefferson said, "The many!"
Hamilton said, "The few!"
Like opposite sides of a penny
Were those exalted two.
If Jefferson said, "It's black, sir!"
Hamilton cried, "It's white!"
But, 'twixt the two, our Constitu-
    tion started working right.

Hamilton liked the courtly,
Jefferson liked the plain,
They'd bow for a while, but shortly
The fight would break out again.

H. was the stripling Colonel
That Washington loved and knew,
A man of mark with a burning spark
Before he was twenty-two.

He came from the warm Antilles
Where the love and the hate last long,
And he thought most people sillies
Who should be ruled by the strong.
Brilliant, comely and certain,
He generally got his way,
—Till the sillies said, "We'd rather be dead."
And then it was up to J.

He could handle the Nation's dollars
With a magic that's known to few,
He could talk with wits and scholars
And scratch like a wildcat, too.
And he yoked the States together
With a yoke that is strong and stout.
(It was common dust that he did not trust
And that's where J. wins out.)

His mind was as clear as crystal.
He dined from a silver plate.
And he died by Aaron's pistol
Before he was forty-eight.
With his face unmarred by the bullet,
They looked at him, lying dead—
"There's a comet bright in the skies tonight,"
Betsey Hamilton said.

AARON BURR

1756-1836

"O, Aaron Burr, what have you done?
You've shot great General Hamilton!
You hid behind a bunch of thistles
And shot him dead with two horse-pistols!"

O, Aaron Burr, alack the day!
It is not right, such men to slay!
He took some snuff, he smiled a smile.
He went to Blennerhassett's isle.

And there he planned a deed of night
—Or else, perhaps, it wasn't quite—
A dire and deadly, doleful plot
—Though some historians think not.

It was to draw his snickersnee
—Or sheathe it, as the case may be—
And carve a Western Empire new
(He said that wasn't quite his view).

For Aaron Burr was bold and bad
—Or else a deeply injured lad—
And all his deeds were false and sly—
—Or someone's told a whopping lie.

He shot great Hamilton, 'tis true.
(He had some provocation, too.)
And as Vice-President he sat
(But men are seldom hanged for that).

He hatched such dark and dubious schemes
(His friends all called them "noble dreams"),
They tried him for his treason bold.
(And yet acquitted him, I'm told.)

It was a fearful, fearful deed
(But *what* it was, finds few agreed),
For all his acts were blithe and base
(He had a most attractive face).

O Aaron Burr, you make me frown!
I cannot get your portrait down.
Were you a rascal or a butt,
A spoilt Napoleon or what?

You lived so long, you schemed so much
And yet you always got in Dutch.
No doubt you were a man of guile—
But, as for Blennerhassett's isle,

And what they say you meant to do,
I simply can't tell which from who!
So, read his riddle if you can.
I can't. Confusion on the man!

JOHNNY APPLESEED

1775-1847

Of Jonathan Chapman
Two things are known,
That he loved apples,
That he walked alone.

At seventy-odd
He was gnarled as could be,
But ruddy and sound
As a good apple tree.

For fifty years over
Of harvest and dew,
He planted his apples
Where no apples grew.

The winds of the prairie
Might blow through his rags,
But he carried his seeds
In the best deerskin bags.

From old Ashtabula
To frontier Fort Wayne,
He planted and pruned
And he planted again.

He had not a hat
To encumber his head.
He wore a tin pan
On his white hair instead.

He nested with owl,
And with bear-cub and possum,
And knew all his orchards
Root, tendril and blossom.

A fine old man,
As ripe as a pippin,
His heart still light,
And his step still skipping.

The stalking Indian,
The beast in its lair
Did no hurt
While he was there.

For they could tell,
As wild things can,
That Jonathan Chapman
Was God's own man.

Why did he do it?
We do not know.
He wished that apples
Might root and grow.

He has no statue.
He has no tomb.
He has his apple trees
Still in bloom.

Consider, consider,
Think well upon
The marvelous story
Of Appleseed John.

LEWIS AND CLARK
1774-1809   1770-1838

Lewis and Clark
Said, "Come on, let's embark
For a boating trip up the Missouri!
It's the President's wish
And we might catch some fish,
Though the river is muddy as fury."

So they started away
On a breezy May day,
Full of courage and lore scientific,
And, before they came back,
They had blazed out a track
From St. Louis straight to the Pacific.

Now, if *you* want to go
From St. Louis (in Mo.)
To Portland (the Ore. not the Me. one),
You can fly there in planes
Or board limited trains
Or the family car, if there be one.

It may take you two weeks,
If your car's full of squeaks
And you stop for the sights and the strangers,
But it took them (don't laugh!)
Just one year and a half,
Full of buffalo, Indians and dangers.

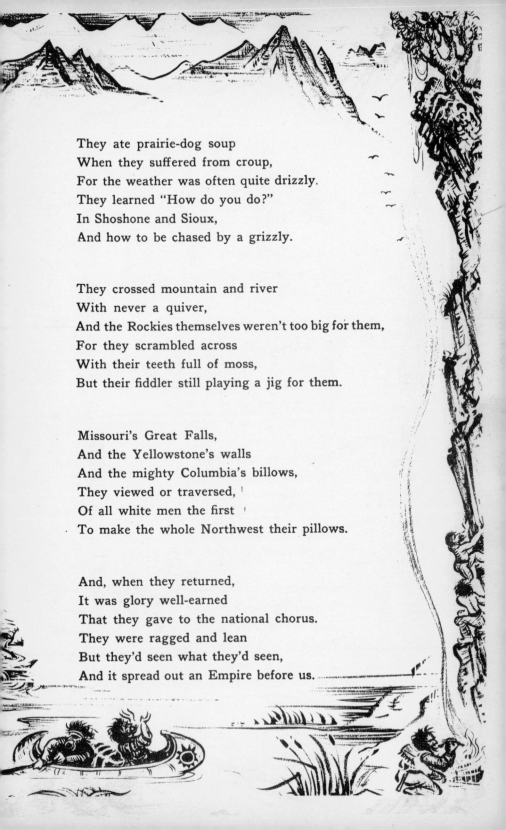

They ate prairie-dog soup
When they suffered from croup,
For the weather was often quite drizzly.
They learned "How do you do?"
In Shoshone and Sioux,
And how to be chased by a grizzly.

They crossed mountain and river
With never a quiver,
And the Rockies themselves weren't too big for them,
For they scrambled across
With their teeth full of moss,
But their fiddler still playing a jig for them.

Missouri's Great Falls,
And the Yellowstone's walls
And the mighty Columbia's billows,
They viewed or traversed,
Of all white men the first
To make the whole Northwest their pillows.

And, when they returned,
It was glory well-earned
That they gave to the national chorus.
They were ragged and lean
But they'd seen what they'd seen,
And it spread out an Empire before us.

DOLLY MADISON

1772-1849

Dolly Madison
(Dorothea Payne),
Married, was widowed
And married again.

Passing by other
More dashing names
To set her cap
For "the great little" James.

She loved fine clothes,
Though she was a Quaker.
She wore linen masks
So the sun wouldn't bake her.

Her eyes were large,
Her manners urban,
And she posed for her portrait
Wearing a turban.

She brushed her satins,
Tended her beauty,
Smoothed her laces,
Minded her duty.

But, though fine and grand
On her at-home day,
She could still take snuff
With Henry Clay.

When the British began
To cut more capers
And burned the White House,
She didn't have vapors.

The roofs fell in
And the cut-glass burst—
But she saved George Washington's
Portrait first.

She didn't talk much.
She eschewed all tears.
She went to a ball
At fourscore years.

But her very last words
Set us staring—for—
"There's nothing in this life
Worth caring for."

Said by a lady
Who loved her life
And, more than most,
Was a perfect wife,

Make us wonder a little,
Though with no stigma,
If Dolly·could have been
An enigma.

JAMES MONROE

1758-1831

James Monroe, James Monroe,
What is there about him I ought to know?
He wasn't a buck, he wasn't a beau,
He was tall and plain, he was grave and slow,
(Though his eyes, they say, had "a kindly glow")
He was Jefferson's friend and Hamilton's foe.
He fought in the army and studied law
But his favorite oath was probably "Pshaw!"
He went to France, but, alack, alack,
He talked behind his government's back
And they called him home with a flea in his ear
For Washington thought him quite small beer,
And the Federalists and all their ilk
Called him "James the Second" and "Water-and-Milk,"
For he wasn't wild and he wasn't tame
But he got to be President just the same
And stayed eight years in the White House, too,
Which is more than many Presidents do.

And when he was there,
In the President's chair,
The times, on the whole, weren't very exciting
In the obvious ways of wars and fighting,
Though lots of things were starting and changing
And the bold frontiersmen kept on ranging
And Florida was bought from the Spanish
And men's hair-powder began to vanish
—And the fuse was laid to the powder-store
That would burst, in time, in Civil War—
But, when men looked round
They generally found
The times had a rather peaceful sound,
So, in spite of the usual grumbling and squealing,
They called it "The Era of Good Feeling,"
And, up in the White House, sat James Monroe—

But what *is* there about him I ought to *know?*

Well, he did one thing you shouldn't forget
For he put up a sign that is standing yet,
A sign on the Western Hemisphere,
"THESE COUNTRIES ARE SETTLED. NO PARKING
     HERE."

Which meant, in language clear and plain,
To England, Russia, France and Spain
And all the rest of Europe, too:
"We do not care what else you do.
But keep your little hands away
From North and South Amerikay.
We love you dearly, understand,
But—just refrain from claiming land
Between Cape Horn and Baffin's Bay
Or there will be the deuce to pay.

We like your martial grenadiers,
Your cossacks, uhlans, cuirassiers,
While they are merely forming squares
But, should they land at Buenos Aires
Or march on Bogota or Quito,
You'll find you've slapped the wrong mosquito!
With what you have, we have no quarrel.
We only draw one simple moral
From Labrador to Darien
And South to Horn and back again,
'These gates are shut. Respect these gates.'
Yours truly,
                The United States."

So *that's* what he did! Why, James Monroe!
Yes, he did it all right. And we still say so.

JOHN QUINCY ADAMS

1767-1848

When President John Quincy
Set out to take a swim,
He'd hang his Presidential clothes
Upon a hickory limb,
And bound in the Potomac
Like a dolphin on the swell.
—He was extremely dignified
But rather plump, as well.

And when Supreme Court Justices
Remarked, from a canoe,
"Our Presidents don't do such things."
He merely said, "I do."
He never asked what people thought
But gave them tit for tat.
—The Adamses have always been
Remarkably like that.

ANDREW JACKSON

1767-1845

The East and the South have ruled us long
And they mean to keep on ruling,
But the wild boy West is growing strong
And tired of their constant schooling.
He carries a rifle, long and brown,
And his rough, free ways they fear.
But here comes
Old Hickory,
The pride of the frontier.

He's none of your old New England stock,
Or your gentry-proud Virginians,
But a regular Western fighting-cock
With Tennessee opinions.
When the gathered West, at New Orleans,
Mowed down the grenadier,
Who led the fight?
Old Hickory!
The pride of the frontier.

He was born and raised like a young raccoon
In the midst of death and dangers,
And his hair may be white as the hunter's moon
But his eyes are the forest-ranger's.
"This country's bigger than East or South.
Old ways must disappear.
Let the people rule!"
Says Hickory
"As they rule on the frontier!"

They follow behind him, the lusty crew
Of the States with the Injun trophies.
They'll sweep him into the White House, too,
And cock their boots on the sofys.
The rich and the staid may ring their hands
But how the people cheer!
To see him there,
Old Hickory,
The pride of the frontier.

ZACHARY TAYLOR
1784-1850

Zachary Taylor was gallant and gruff,
A general rugged and heady,
He fought like a trump in the Mexican war
And his troops called him "Old Rough and Ready."
For he didn't much mind if their buttons weren't shined
As long as no man was a quailer
And the Mexicans found that their best bit the ground
When faced by old Zachary Taylor.

Zachary Taylor was President T.
One very warm day in July,
When he called for a bowl of ripe cherries and milk,
With a greedy old gleam in his eye,
Now, cherries and milk, when the weather is hot,
Make even the strongest turn paler
—And they proved more effective than Mexican shot
For they finished poor Zachary Taylor.

JOHN JAMES AUDUBON

1780-1851

Some men live for warlike deeds,
Some for women's words.
John James Audubon
Lived to look at birds.

Pretty birds and funny birds,
All our native fowl
From the little cedar waxwing
To the Great Horned Owl.

Let the wind blow hot or cold,
Let it rain or snow,
Everywhere the birds went
Audubon would go.

Scrambling through a wilderness,
Floating down a stream,
All around America
In a feathered dream.

Thirty years of traveling,
Pockets often bare,
(Lucy Bakewell Audubon
Patched them up with care).

Followed grebe and meadowlark,
Saw them sing and splash.
(Lucy Bakewell Audubon
Somehow raised the cash).

Drew them all the way they lived
In their habitats.
(Lucy Bakewell Audubon
Sometimes wondered "Cats?")

Colored them and printed them
In a giant book,
"Birds of North America"—
All the world said, "Look!"

Gave him medals and degrees,
Called him noble names,
—Lucy Bakewe'' Audubon
Kissed her queer John James.

NANCY HANKS

1784-1818

If Nancy Hanks
Came back as a ghost,
Seeking news
Of what she loved most,
She'd ask first
"Where's my son?
What's happened to Abe?
What's he done?

"Poor little Abe,
Left all alone
Except for Tom,
Who's a rolling stone;
He was only nine
The year I died.
I remember still
How hard he cried.

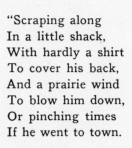

"Scraping along
In a little shack,
With hardly a shirt
To cover his back,
And a prairie wind
To blow him down,
Or pinching times
If he went to town.

"You wouldn't know
About my son?
Did he grow tall?
Did he have fun?
Did he learn to read?
Did he get to town?
Do you know his name?
Did he get on?"

DANIEL BOONE

1735-1820

When Daniel Boone goes by, at night,
The phantom deer arise
And all lost, wild America
Is burning in their eyes.

CRAWFORD LONG AND
WILLIAM MORTON

1815-1878   1819-1868

"O, whet your saws and shine your knives,
Ye surgeons, tried and true!
We're going for to operate
In eighteen-forty-two!

"And, if the patient starts to yell
And bounce about the floor,
Just tell him Pain is bound to be,
And give him one chop more!"

A doctor down in Georgia,
His name was Crawford Long,
Began to wonder, more or less,
About this little song.

"The words," he said, "are elegant.
I like the gay refrain.
But, mightn't there be something in
Abolishing the pain?"

And, up in windy Boston town,
A dentist, bold but kind,
Named William Morton, felt the same
Idea tease his mind.

They didn't know each other from
An inlay or a pill,
But both found out, without a doubt,
That ether filled the bill.

For once a man's anesthetized
And ether's work begins,
You'll sleep without an ouch, although
They stick you full of pins.

To Long belongs priority
In this historic boon,
But Morton was the man who made
The surgeons change their tune.

At Massachusetts General
He showed it to the nation.
—And everybody gaped to see
A painless operation.

For Man had suffered and endured
And Man had racked his brain.
But, till those two, no creature knew
The knife without the pain.

SAM HOUSTON

1793-1863

Whenever Sam Houston felt ill at ease
He'd go and live with the Cherokees,
For he liked their ways and he liked their dress
And the free, proud life of the wilderness.

This buckskin hero from Tennessee
Had a life as checkered as lives can be.
There was speech and duel and love and ire,
And all of it lived like a prairie fire.

He was up and down, he was hissed and cheered,
But there was never anything Houston feared.
His dreams were huge and his costumes showy
And his private honor bright as a bowie.

He's the pride and boast of the Lone Star State
For he fought her battles and made her great,
And, on either side of the wide Atlantic,
You won't find anyone more romantic.

WESTERN WAGONS

They went with axe and rifle, when the trail was still to blaze,
They went with wife and children, in the prairie-schooner days,
With banjo and with frying pan—Susanna, don't you cry!
For I'm off to California to get rich out there or die!

We've broken land and cleared it, but we're tired of where
    we are.
They say that wild Nebraska is a better place by far.
There's gold in far Wyoming, there's black earth in Ioway,
So pack up the kids and blankets, for we're moving out today!

The cowards never started and the weak died on the road,
And all across the continent the endless campfires glowed.
We'd taken land and settled—but a traveler passed by—
And we're going West tomorrow—Lordy, never ask us why!

We're going West tomorrow, where the promises can't fail.
O'er the hills in legions, boys, and crowd the dusty trail!
We shall starve and freeze and suffer. We shall die, and tame
the lands.
But we're going West tomorrow, with our fortune in our
hands.

CLIPPER SHIPS AND CAPTAINS

1843-1860

There was a time before our time,
It will not come again,
When the best ships still were wooden ships
But the men were iron men.

From Stonington to Kennebunk
The Yankee hammers plied
To build the clippers of the wave
That were New England's pride.

The "Flying Cloud," the "Northern Light,"
The "Sovereign of the Seas"
—There was salt music in the blood
That thought of names like these.

"Sea Witch," "Red Jacket," "Golden Age"
And "Chariot of Fame,"
The whole world gaped to look at them
Before the steamship came.

Their cargoes were of tea and gold,
Their bows a cutting blade,
And, on the bridge, the skippers walked,
Lords of the China trade.

The skippers with the little beards
And the New England drawl
Who knew Hong Kong and Marblehead
And the Pole Star over all.

Stately as churches, swift as gulls,
They trod the oceans, then—
No man had seen such ships before
And none will see again.

JAMES BUCHANAN

1791-1868

Poor James Buchanan!
He didn't know what to do,
For the South was getting its dander up
And the North was angry, too.

"You're villains and knaves for holding slaves!"
The Abolitionists groan,
But the Southerners swear it's their own affair
And the North must leave it alone.

Poor James Buchanan:
He fiddled and fussed and blew,
While the argument went from bad to worse
As arguments often do.
"We'd rather be done with the Union
Than let you Yankees boss us!"
"You Southerners crow you're the whole blame show,
But just you try to cross us!"

It was "Shan't!" and "Won't!" and "Can't!" and "Don't!"
And "Liar!" and "You're another!"
Till the whole wide land was split in two
And brother set against brother,
Till, at last, with a "There!" and a haughty stare,
In martial precipitation,
The Southern States left the Union's gates
To set up a separate nation.

Poor James Buchanan!
He twiddled his four years through,
And left the mess for somebody else
As weak men always do.
For when times are dark and the outlook stark,
The government needs a man on
Its chair of State, not an addlepate
Like weary old James Buchanan.

CRAZY HORSE

?-1877

The Indians of the Wild West
We found were hard to tame,
For they seemed really quite possessed
To keep their ways the same.

They liked to hunt, they liked to fight,
And (this I grieve to say)
They could not see the white man's right
To take their land away.

So there was fire upon the Plains,
And deeds of derring-do,
Where Sioux were bashing soldier's brains
And soldiers bashing Sioux'.

And here is bold Chief Crazy Horse,
A warrior, keen and tried,
Who fought with fortitude and force
—But on the losing side.

Where Custer fell, where Miles pursued,
He led his native sons,
And did his best, though it was crude
And lacked the Gatling guns.

It was his land. They were his men.
He cheered and led them on.
—The hunting ground is pasture, now.
The buffalo are gone.

STONEWALL JACKSON

1824-1863

"Fool Tom" Jackson
Aren't you tired of teaching,
Teaching boys tactics
In a dusty study hall?
"I read Napoleon's Maxims
And the Book of Kings and Prophets.
I hear a wind rising
I wait for a call."

T. J. Jackson,
Bible in your saddle-bags,
Surely you're an odd man
To be a general?
—First Bull Run.
The battle reels and wavers.
"Rally behind Jackson!
He stands like a stone wall!"

Stonewall Jackson,
Hammer of the Valley,
Lee's right arm
And a very famous man.
—"Old Jack's here, boys!
Now we'll see some action!
God help the Yanks,
When he prays the way he can!"

Stonewall Jackson,
After his last battle,
Wounded to the death,
What is it that he sees?
What do you say
Now the hard toil is ending?
"Let us cross the river
And rest beneath the trees."

ABRAHAM LINCOLN

1809-1865

Lincoln was a long man.
He liked out of doors.
He liked the wind blowing
And the talk in country stores.

He liked telling stories,
He liked telling jokes.
"Abe's quite a character,"
Said quite a lot of folks.

Lots of folks in Springfield
Saw him every day,
Walking down the street
In his gaunt, long way.

Shawl around his soulders,
Letters in his hat.
"That's Abe Lincoln."
They thought no more than that.

Knew that he was honest,
Guessed that he was odd,
Knew he had a cross wife
Though she was a Todd.

Knew he had three little boys
Who liked to shout and play,
Knew he had a lot of debts
It took him years to pay.

Knew his clothes and knew his house.
"That's his office, here.
Blame good lawyer, on the whole,
Though he's sort of queer.

"Sure, he went to Congress, once,
But he didn't stay.
Can't expect us all to be
Smart as Henry Clay.

"Need a man for troubled times?
Well, I guess we do.
Wonder who we'll ever find?
Yes—I wonder who."

That is how they met and talked,
Knowing and unknowing.
Lincoln was the green pine.
Lincoln kept on growing.

NEGRO SPIRITUALS

We do not know who made them.
The lips that gave them birth
Are dust in the slaves' burying ground,
Anonymous as earth.

The poets, the musicians,
Were bondsmen bred and born.
They picked the master's cotton,
They hoed the master's corn.

The load was heavy on their backs,
The way was long and cold,
—But out of stolen Africa,
The singing river rolled,
And David's hands were dusky hands,
But David's harp was gold.

ULYSSES S. GRANT

1822-1885

Ulysses was a soldier
And a soldier great was he,
He bested every foe he faced,
Including Robert Lee.

Ulysses was a gentleman,
Although not always neat.
He wouldn't take Lee's sword away
After Lee's defeat.

Ulysses was an honest man
But friends could get around him,
—And so, when he was President,
A poorish one we found him.

It works that way, sometimes, I fear,
For men are kittle cattle.
—How many rhymers, children dear,
Have ever won a battle?

ROBERT E. LEE

1807-1870

This is Lee of the battles,
Virginia's bright star,
The sword of the South,
Through the long Civil War.

Of family noted
And most F. F. V.,
A dauntless and chivalrous
Leader was he.

He vanquished McClellan
And Hooker and Pope.
He trimmed poor old Burnside
Of whiskers and hope.

The pride of the armies
Who strove for the grey,
He was never defeated
Till Gettysburg's day.

But Meade was the horseshoe
He didn't quite bend—
And then came Ulysses
S. Grant—and the end.

The end of the war
And the fall of the South
And wild, bitter counsels
From many a mouth.

They looked to Marse Robert
To see what he'd say.
He looked at his sword
And he put it away.

He said, "We have fought.
We have lost. Let it stand.
Forget the old rancors
And work for your land.

"Put your heart to the task
And your hand to the plow.
The war days are over.
We're one country, now."

And he spent the last years
Of his life as the head
Of Washington College
And taught for his bread.

While, all through the South,
The quick whispering ran,
"If Marse Robert does it,
I reckon we can."

DAVID GLASGOW FARRAGUT

1801-1870

"Damn the torpedoes!"
Bold Farragut said,
"Damn the torpedoes!
Full speed ahead!"

And, lashed to his rigging
With never a squeal,
He led his fleet into
The Bay of Mobile.

The Southern forts thundered
With vigor and vim
But grapeshot and canister
Never touched him.

The waters were mined
With a death-dealing load,
But Farragut simply
Refused to explode.

And fought till the Southerners
Gave up the fray.
(He'd captured New Orleans
In much the same way.)

So remember, if ever
You face such a plight,
There's a pretty good chance,
"Straight ahead!" will be right.

And while "damn," as you know,
Is a word to eschew—
He knew when to say it—
So few people do.

CLARA BARTON

(1821-1912)

Brave Clara Barton
Stood beside her door,
And watched young soldiers
March away to war.

"The flags are very fine," she said,
"The drums and trumpets thrilling.
But what about the wounds
When the guns start killing?"

Clara Barton went to work
To help keep men alive,
And never got a moment's rest
Till eighteen-sixty-five.

She washed and she bandaged,
She shooed away the flies,
She hurried in nurses,
She begged for supplies.

She cared for the wounded
And comforted the dying,
With no time for sleep
And still less for crying.

Clara Barton went abroad
When the war was ended.
Hoping for a little peace
Now that things had mended.

Clara found, as soon,
As her foot touched shore,
That she'd come just in time
For the Franco-Prussian War.

After that, her life, for her,
Held but little rest,
With famine in the East
And earthquakes in the West.

Floods, drowning Johnstown,
Hurricanes in Texas,
Fires, out in Michigan,
Things that fright and vex us.

In between the hurry calls,
Never at a loss,
She founded and established
The merciful Red Cross.

Battle, murder, sudden death,
Called for Clara Barton.
No one ever called in vain.
Clara was a Spartan.

DANIEL DREW

1797-1879

O, Daniel Drew, O, Daniel Drew
I shiver when I think of you!

This sanctimonious old sneak
Pretended to be poor and meek,
But all he cared for, first and last,
Was making money just as fast
As he could get it in his claws,
In spite of justice, right or laws.
He toiled not, neither did he spin,
But how he raked the dollars in!
(The process suffers various changes
But still occurs, on Stock Exchanges,
Where there are things called bulls and bears.
And people sell what isn't theirs
To buy Amalgamated Pup
Because they think it's going up,
And then, with quite a sickly frown,
Find out it's really going down.
They didn't know, but someone knew
And someone got the money, too,
Someone, in fact. like Daniel Drew),
Who, in his time, was known as a
Financial wizard of the day,
And, like a pious basilisk,
With sleek Jay Gould and blithe Jim Fisk,
Made other people's money fly
And sucked the Erie Railroad dry.
They foiled the laws, they bribed the courts,
They watered stock, they squeezed the shorts.

In fact, the various things they did
Make one regret poor Captain Kidd,
Who merely scuttled, robbed and burned
And got the hanging that he earned.
They stole on a much larger scale
And didn't even go to jail.
And, of the whole piratic crew,
The meanest one was Daniel Drew,
Until, at last, I'm glad to say,
Gould put the screws on *him* one day,
And drained him of his ill-got hoard
And dumped him gaily overboard
To sink or swim at eighty-two.
"I'll die at par!" cried Daniel Drew,
But, fortunately, died before
He had a chance to steal some more.

Why rake from history's dirt and damp
The memory of this tarnished scamp?
Why, Daniel Drew, why, Daniel Drew,
It makes me ill to think of you.
But there were lots of others, too . . .
And there are still some others, too . . . .

JESSE JAMES

1847-1882

Among our country's outlaws
There are some lusty names,
But many a voice would make a choice
Of Jesse Woodson James.

No wishy-washy man was he
Of milk and *aqua pura*.
He shook the ground for miles around
His native soil, Mizzoura.

"Allow me!" said his brother,
His helpful partner, Frank.
Then out they'd sail to rob the mail
Or polish off a bank.

The sheriffs found, unlike the hound,
His bite worse than his bark.
He shot as well as William Tell
Though apples weren't his mark.

And those who came to spoil his game
Found people sometimes coy.
For lots would say, "It's Jesse's way.
He's just a home-town boy."

"They done him wrong when he was young.
Perhaps he should have borne it.
But we have found it is not sound
To step upon a hornet."

He robbed and looted banks and trains.
He took what wasn't his'n.
He thumbed his nose at all of those
Who sadly muttered, "Prison!"

A price was put upon his head.
His luck began to crack.
Two of his men turned traitor then
And shot him in the back.

Jesse died at thirty-five,
Frank lived to threescore-ten.
Of their kind you will not find
Two more daring men.

Some call Jess Missouri's pride,
Some say he's her shame,
All we can say is, anyway
He earned his outlaw fame.

GROVER CLEVELAND

1837-1908

Stephen Grover Cleveland
Was a minister's son,
And named for a minister,
Although he wasn't one.

A big boy, a sturdy boy,
He liked to fight and skate.
He worked hard and played hard
Early days and late.

He liked broiled steaks
And he didn't sniff at sinners.
He wasn't much for angel cake
Or dress-suit dinners.

Strong as a cart horse,
Dogged as the tide,
Cleveland was the sort of man
It's hard to push aside.

Lots of hungry gentlemen
Go in politics.
Lots of politicians
Have lots of little tricks.

When a Cleveland comes along,
Goodness, how they squeal!
Cleveland called a thief a thief,
He called a steal a steal.

Popular? Unpopular?
Cleveland didn't care.
Once he put his big hand down,
It stayed right there.

President, Ex-President,
President again,
They cursed him, they praised him,
He didn't change a grain.

Politicians watch the votes.
Politicians can.
Cleveland went his own way.
Cleveland was a man.

P. T. BARNUM

1810-1891

Come see the two-horned jigamaree
And the gen-uine mermaid rare!
The elephants in their Sunday pants
And the dangerous polar bear!
This way, this way, for the freaks at play
And the cold pink lemonade!
For Barnum's fooling the world again!
Barnum's on parade!

O, tootle the rope of the callyope!
Whang on the big bass drum!
Let the welkin ring for the Showman King
And General Tom Thumb!
For Jenny Lind of the musical wind
And Jumbo, London's pride,
And all of the Greatest Show On Earth
Ere P. T. Barnum died!

For freaks were the joy of this Bethel boy,
And he knew folks paid to see 'em,
And anything new they'd troop to view
In his marvelous Dime Museum.
By hook or crook, he would make them look
If he had to bloom like a crocus.
O, the marvelous lies that Barnum told!
The wonderful hocus-pocus!

Walk in, walk in, let the show begin!
Don't let those children wait!
The lions snort and the clowns cavort
And Barnum stands by the gate.
His Yankee eyes are merry with lies,
He's telling a gilded story.
O, the marvelous show that Barnum gave
In his humbug days of glory!

WALTER REED

1851-1902

"O, Yellow Jack's here,
With his yellow flag flying.
And everywhere, everywhere,
People are dying.
Our doctors and nurses
Work on till they fall,
But he stings us and slays us,
In spite of them all!

"He scourges the tropics
And all the warm South,
But the North has been seared
By the breath of his mouth.
What might shall withstand him?
What skill drive away
The dread yellow fever
That sickens the day?"

It was not a wizard,
With philters and charms,
It was not a champion,
A champion-at-arms,
But a lean army surgeon,
Soft-spoken and slight,
Who read the dark riddle
And broke the dark might.

He found the mosquito
That carried the pest,
He called volunteers
For a terrible test.
They walked in Death's valley,
—And one, to Death's door—
But Yellow Jack, Yellow Jack
Slaughters no more!

There is valor in battle
And statues for those
Who pepper and puncture
Our national foes—
But, if you are looking
For heroes to cheer,
You needn't look farther
Than Reed and Lazear.

WILBUR WRIGHT AND
ORVILLE WRIGHT

1867-1912   1871-

Said Orville Wright to Wilbur Wright,
"These birds are very trying.
I'm sick of hearing them cheep-cheep
About the fun of flying.
A bird has feathers, it is true.
That much I freely grant.
But, must that stop us, W?"
Said Wilbur Wright, "It shan't."

And so they built a glider, first,
And then they built another.
—There never were two brothers more
Devoted to each other.
They ran a dusty little shop
For bicycle-repairing,
And bought each other soda-pop
And praised each other's daring.

They glided here, they glided there,
They sometimes skinned their noses,
—For learning how to rule the air
Was not a bed of roses—
But each would murmur, afterward,
While patching up his bro.
"Are we discouraged, W?"
"Of course we are not, O!"

And finally, at Kitty Hawk
In Nineteen-Three (let's cheer it!),
The first real airplane really flew
With Orville there to steer it!
—And kingdoms may forget their kings
And dogs forget their bites,
But, not till Man forgets his wings,
Will men forget the Wrights.

ROBERT PEARY

1856-1920

The far North Pole, upon the whole,
Sounds cold to me and dreary,
But there are those who love its floes,
Though few like Robert Peary.

He liked a meal of frozen seal
At forty below zero
(It takes a tum that naught can numb
To be an Arctic hero).

He loved to snooze in damp igloos
Lit by a lamp of blubber,
(It gives a light that lasts all night,
But smells like burning rubber).

The Eskimos had chilblained toes,
The Northern Lights were eerie.
But did he flinch or yield an inch?
You don't know Robert Peary.

The Arctic wind was bleak and blind,
The Arctic ice was gritty,
But Peary's soul besieged the Pole
As men besiege a city.

For eighteen years of hopes and fears
He quested and he sought it,
Until, by Gum! the day had come
And Peary murmured, "Got it!"

"The real North Pole? God bless my soul!
You're looking well and cheerful!"
The Pole (they're shy) would not reply
But seemed a little tearful.

THEODORE ROOSEVELT

1858-1919

T. R. is spanking a Senator,
T. R. is chasing a bear,
T. R. is busting an Awful Trust
And dragging it from its lair.
They're calling T. R. a lot of things
—The men in the private car—
But the day-coach likes exciting folks
And the day-coach likes T. R.

T. R. is having a bully time.
His hat's in every ring.
He's shooting lions in Africa.
He's shaking hands with a king.
He's writing books and he's biting crooks,
And his Big Stick swings afar.
No, it isn't really the Judgment Day,
It's simply our T. R.

I wouldn't call him infallible,
But you can understand
Why life was never a dull affair
When T. R. ruled the land.
We've had quite a lot of Presidents,
They come from near and far,
—And few have tried to avoid the job—
—A couple merely annoyed the job—
But no one ever enjoyed the job
With the gusto of T. R.

111

WOODROW WILSON

1856-1924

When Wilson was a little boy
His friends all called him Tommy,
And so did all his relatives,
His father and his mommy.

But, when he grew to man's estate,
"Tommy," he thought, might be
Not quite the name for anyone
As scholarly as he.

And so it's Woodrow Wilson, who
Is known to us and fame,
And I admire him hugely but
Why *did* he slice his name?

There's Thomas Moore and Thomas Paine,
And Thomas (St.) who doubted,
And all of them were men of brain
And none their Thomas flouted.

There's Thomas Rhymer, Tommy Green,
And Thomas called Aquinas.
They always thought of Thomas plus
And not of Thomas minus.

While Woodrow, though a name of worth,
Is somewhat awe-inspiring,
I wonder if he ever found
Its weight a trifle tiring?

He rowed the storm-tossed barque of State
As well as any could row.
—But Tommy Wilson had the fun—
Well, well, he would choose Woodrow.

U. S. A.

So we march into the present
And it's always rather pleasant
To speculate on what the years ahead of us will see,
For our words and thoughts and attitudes,
All our novelties and platitudes,
Will be Rather Ancient History in 2033.

Will they find us wise—or silly?
Looking backwards, willy-nilly,
At our queer old-fashioned costumes and our quaint old-fash-
    ioned ways?
When our doings face the ages,
Printed down on textbook pages,
Will they cry, "This Savage Era"? Will they sigh, "Those were
    the days!"?

I don't know—you may be wiser.
Time's a curious capsizer
Of a lot of reputations that seemed certain to endure,
While he'll sometimes make his heroes
Out of people, once thought zeroes,
For the most well-grounded reasons, by the solemnly cocksure.

So, instead of prophesying
(Which is fun, but rather trying)
Who they'll pick to be our great ones when the books are on
    the shelves,
Here's the marching panorama
Of our past and present drama
—And we shan't know all the answers till we're history,
    ourselves.